COLORADO FOURTEENERS
GRAND SLAM

Photography, Text and Maps by

ROGER EDRINN

Fort Collins, Colorado

Durango · Animas River · El Diente Peak · Mount Wilson · Wilson Peak · San Miguel River · 550 · Mount Sneffels · 62 · Ouray · 550 · Montrose · Mount Eolus · Windom Peak · Sunlight Peak · Handies Peak · Wetterhorn Peak · Redcloud Peak · Uncompahgre Peak · Sunshine Peak · Lake City · San Juan River · Wolf Creek Pass · Creede · San Luis Peak · 149 · Blue Mesa Re · Gunnison · Rio Grande · 50 · 160 · Monte Vista · 114 · Mount Antero · Mount Har · Alamosa · San Luis Valley · 285 · Saguache · Mount Tabeguache · Mount Yale · Mount Shavano · Little Bear Peak · Ellingwood Point · Mount Princeton · Mount Colu · 159 · Blanca Peak · Great Sand Dunes NM · 17 · Kit Carson Mountain · Salida · 285 · Buena Vista · Mount Lindsey · Crestone Needle · Crestone Peak · Culebra Peak · Humboldt Peak · Arkansas River · Spanish Peaks · Westcliffe · South Park · 69 · 50 · Walsenburg · Canon City · 24 · Huerfano River · 115 · 9 · Pueblo · South Plate River · 25 · Pikes Peak · BILL C. BROWN · Colorado Springs

Grand Junction

70

Gunnison River

Snowmass Mountain
Maroon Peak   Capitol Peak   Mount Sopris
Pyramid Peak   North Maroon Peak   Glenwood Springs
astle Peak

ron Peak   Aspen   Colorado River
              82

La Plata Peak
Mount Elbert
ssouri Mountain   Mount Massive   Mount of the Holy Cross
unt Belford
unt Oxford   Eagle River
              24
Mount Sherman   Leadville

Mount Democrat   Vail
Mount Lincoln   Quandary Peak
Mount Bross
                  Breckenridge   Blue River   Kremmling
Fairplay
                                    6   40
              285
              Grays Peak   Torreys Peak
Kenosha Pass   Granby
        Mount Bierstadt
            Mount Evans
                                                        Front Range   Rocky Mountain National Park
                          103
                    Idaho Springs   Longs Peak

                                                                        Estes Park
                    70

                    Golden

                                Boulder

                                                                                34
Denver
                              25
                                                              Loveland

Contents

Maps

Disclaimer

Climbing mountains can be dangerous. The author assumes no liability for the actions of any reader. While the attempt has been made to be accurate, the directions may contain errors of fact. Almost certainly directions can be misinterpreted. It is impossible for the author to anticipate all the various skill levels of people who might purchase this book. Therefore, the author does not offer this book to the consumer for any purpose other than pleasure reading.

Copyright: Photographs © 1985-1990, Text & Maps © 1991, by Roger Edrinn

Published by: Above the Timber, 2366 Wapiti Road, Fort Collins, Colorado 80525

Publishing Consultants: SkyHouse Publishers, an imprint of
Falcon Press Publishing Co., Inc., Helena, Montana

Design: Roger Edrinn and Laurie gigette Gould
Page Layout: Roger Edrinn
Printed by: South Sea International Press, Ltd., Hong Kong

Library of Congress Catalog Card Number: 91-70371
ISBN 1-56044-087-2

Front Cover: Beauty and the Beast. The reader is left to his or her own imagination whether the flowering thistle is beast or beauty, or if Crestone Needle is beauty or beast.

Title Page: A distant moody Longs Peak is framed by the glowing buttresses of the Rock Cut at sunset.

Pages 2 and 3: Painting of Colorado's Mountains provided courtesy of Coors Brewing Company. © 1982, 1990.

Facing Page: The splendor of fall along East Dallas Creek when scrub oak turns crimson, aspen golden and Mount Sneffels dominates the azure Colorado sky.

The Book

Why climb a fourteener? Is it the satisfaction of doing what few of your peers have done, or a love of the mountains and an excuse to be among Colorado's highest? For me, the answer used to be the challenge and satisfaction of doing what few others had done. Then after climbing the fourteeners a second time I discovered a new meaning to climbing. I found I had mountain disease, a longing for the mountains after a short absence. The fix is more mountains, climbing, skiing, photographing or any other excuse. Therefore, this book is yet another excuse to be in the mountains. The miles of driving, hiking, backpacking, climbing and photographing to do the book were a great source of pleasure. I hope some of that Colorado high I experienced being in the mountains is apparent in these pages and that you too catch the spirit.

Hiking and Climbing

Forget distance if you wish to gauge the difficulty of climbing any mountain. Altitude is by far the better indicator of effort needed to attain a goal. Figure on one hour per thousand feet of elevation gain. This rule of thumb works surprisingly well for a variety of terrains. High quality trails and roads will allow you to double this rate. Steep and/or loose conditions can easily cut it in half. Your personal rate can be defined early and used as a basis for gauging subsequent climbs. Trail conditions and weather are far and away the dominant factors in determining the ease of a climb. The relative difficulty ranking (● ■ ◆ ◆◆) is your best single source to judge potential trail conditions. Forecasting mountain weather is a science and art unto itself. Temperature, wind, rain, snow, and electric storms are all a threat. Another albeit slower acting threat is too much sun. The cool mountain temperatures tend to mask the immediate effects of this high altitude danger. There is no substitute for experience.

Fourteeners and Century Summits

What is a fourteener seems like a dumb question. Obviously, if any piece of rock exceeds 14,000 feet in elevation, at least one fourteener is present. The controversy only begins when a second or third summit is thought to exist. Here is where the arbitrary rules of man are necessary to define the count. The rule, defined by the U.S. Geological Survey and Colorado Mountain Club, is that for a second summit, two conditions must exist: 1) there must be a depression 500 feet below the lower point and 2) the second peak must be at least one mile away. That's easy; now for the exceptions. Several prominent Colorado fourteeners do not qualify based on these rules. Included in this list are two of the hardest: North Maroon and Little Bear. In total six summits out of the fifty-four miss on one or both metrics.

Century or Centennial? Much of the Colorado mountain literature is filled with the term Centennial Peaks, meant to define Colorado's highest hundred summits. Centennial means one hundred years. This text refers to the hundred highest as the Century summits. Incidentally, any summit over 13,800 feet can be thought of as a Century peak.

The Grand Slam Dog

Diente, my canine companion, has accompanied me on virtually all my mountain excursions over the last nine years. His first fourteener was Bierstadt. A fellow hiker asked if he could "make it." Diente was following his usual hundred yards ahead, and I just returned a quizzical nod.

Diente's motivation for being in the mountains is entirely different than mine. While I enjoy the views and exertion, his nose seldom leaves the near vicinity of the ground. Except that is, when any critter about the size of a cat appears. "Any" includes a porcupine—that time I had to remove quills from the roof of his mouth. Brave he may be, not bright.

Two events on his grand slam quest remain most vivid in my mind. 1) While descending Little Bear's steep upper gully (page 40), I let him set his own pace. A section where most climbers rappel and I four-pointed, he went head first and descended in 30 seconds. The revelation from that event was that, unlike humans, dogs can comfortably move head-down. 2) While doing the Wilson–El Diente traverse (page 104), Diente and I were just below the Organ Pipes when the route got very thin. He was on a two inch ledge several feet behind me and I decided to turn back. For whatever reason, I could not get him to turn back. The drop-off was in the neighborhood of thirty feet. As my voice rose, he fell. But rather than fall as you or I would, he pushed off and leapt from one invisible perch to another. Three heart-stopping leaps and he was at the base of the cliff. I immediately called to him as I retraced the route. We met in between. He was dripping blood and my heart stopped again, only to discover he had simply cut his ear. After that we found a lower, safer way around the Organ Pipes to El Diente.

Photography

The equipment I used to take the photos in this book consisted of a 35mm and two medium format cameras. In order of importance were a Horseman VHR 6x9cm roll film field view camera, a Canon A1 35mm SLR, and a Pentax 6x7cm roll film SLR. I have three or more lenses for each camera with an assortment of tripods, light meters and accessories.

Equipment is but a small part of a successful photograph. Most important is the quality of the light, with mid-day sunny light almost the worst. Easily the best is within a hour of sunrise and sunset. This low angle light provides both dramatic shadows to define shape and saturated colors to interest the viewer.

The lush green Huerfano River Basin provides a small beaver pond to reflect the impressive north face of Blanca Peak.

Overleaf: A high thin veil of clouds softens the morning alpenglow on Wilson Peak as seen from Wilson Mesa.

Front Range

When entering Colorado from the east, the Front Range greets the traveler from as far away as 200 miles. This is particularly true on a clear spring morning when the rising sun gleams off the snowcapped summits with that famous Colorado blue sky reaching to the heavens as a backdrop. From north to south many important sub-ranges are included in this major group. To the north are the Medicine Bow and Laramie Mountains and the Mummy Range. To the south are the Rampart Range and the Tarryall and Kenosha Mountains. The Continental Divide follows the ridge of the range in the middle, between the Medicine Bow and Kenosha Mountains. Much of this center portion is called the Indian Peaks, with mountains named after many of the plains Indian tribes.

Six fourteeners are in the Front Range. Two lone sentinels, Longs and Pikes Peaks, are over one hundred miles apart, whereas the core four are less than ten miles apart. For trivia buffs, the Continental Divide in its 500 mile journey through Colorado only crosses over the summits of two of Colorado's fourteeners, those being Grays and Torreys just south of Loveland Pass. Incidentally, Grays Peak is the highest point on the Divide in Canada or America.

The four center summits afford the climber the best opportunity in the state to view mountain goats. These animals are relatively recent additions to Colorado's big game herds. While superbly adapted to Colorado's above timberline heights, some act of Mother Nature banished them from the Southern Rockies millennia ago. Colorado's Division of Wildlife introduced a mixed herd of sixteen to Mount Evans in 1961. The Mount Evans herd now numbers over one hundred animals and ranges from the eastern slopes of Evans to Loveland Pass. Due to relatively light hunting pressure, people can approach these animals easily. Patience works best, inasmuch as these small (28 inches at the shoulders) animals are dwarfed by the average person. Sitting down and allowing their curiosity to overcome natural fear is quite effective. They are particularly attracted to small dogs or children, anything smaller than themselves. Whatever you do, do not surround them. If they feel at all threatened they will flee. Mountain goats can cover steep rocky terrain so fast that in two minutes they will be so many white specks on a distant rocky slope.

Mount Bierstadt and Sawtooth Ridge with the frigid sculpted snows of Guanella Pass in the foreground.

Summit	Elevation	Rank	Page
Longs Peak	14,255	15	13
Mount Evans	14,264	14	15
Mount Bierstadt	14,060	38	15
Torreys Peak	14,267	11	19
Grays Peak	14,270	9	19
Pikes Peak	14,110	31	21

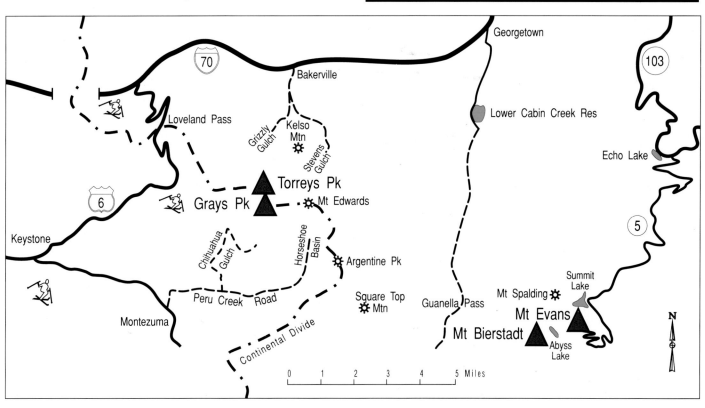

The seldom seen Narrows, between the top of The Trough and the bottom of The Home Stretch, is one of many sources of campfire discussions following a climb of Longs Peak. Notice the climbers and the painted 'fried egg' markers.

Keyhole ◆

A very long, 14 mile round-trip, trail hike with a few exposed sections and frequent three-point climbing after the Keyhole. This is the most scenic of the three routes, especially after the Keyhole.

Cable Route ◆◆

A shorter route compared to the Keyhole, but borderline technical with no route markers. Ice free no more than a few weeks each year.

Loft and Palisades ◆◆

A very difficult, long, off-trail route with several steep sections, some loose rock, exposure, and few people.

Longs Peak

14,255

From the Top: Perhaps the largest summit of all the fourteeners, Longs is surrounded on all sides by steep cliffs. To the west is an unbroken ridge of mountains which form the Continental Divide in northern Colorado. Evidence of the carving power of ice age glaciers can be seen all along this high ridge. Several mountain parks (mountain enclosed meadows) can be seen to the north, including Moraine, Horseshoe and Estes Parks.

The windswept west side of Longs Peak as viewed from a frozen Nymph Lake in Rocky Mountain National Park.

Mount Evans as seen from Summit Lake with a crescent moon at sunset.

Mountain goats relax on a sunny morning on the south slopes of Mount Evans, beyond is Mount Bierstadt.

Guanella Pass (Bierstadt) ●

If you correctly skirt the willows, a two hour easy hike. Otherwise plan on at least an hour of willow-bashing frustration before starting.

Guanella Pass (Evans) ■

A beautiful off-trail hike through grassy meadows, tarns and great views. This short trip through the Mount Evans Wilderness Area offers some of the best scenery in Colorado.

Summit Lake (Evans) ●

Any number of routes are possible from Summit Lake, 12,830 feet. The easiest would be to hike to the east ridge and follow it to the summit. Another possibility is to go west over Mount Spalding, 13,842 feet, and then follow Evans' west ridge to the summit.

Echo Lake (Evans) ●

Bicycle the 14.5 miles from Echo Lake, 10,597 feet, parking area to the summit. This would be a particularly good choice when the road is closed to motor vehicles but still snow-free. Needless to say, this would make for a fabulous fast descent.

Mount Evans

14,264

From the Top: The only paved road above 14,000 feet in the country automatically makes this summit unique. Longs Peak to the north is easily visible due to its block-like top. Pikes Peak can be seen SSE. But the best view has to be of Denver at night with its millions of stationary and moving lights.

Mount Bierstadt

14,060

From the Top: The twin summits of Grays and Torreys help to define the Continental Divide to the west. Further left, if there is still snow on the high peaks, the namesake snowfield of Holy Cross can be seen on the western horizon. Keep turning to see the vast expanse of South Park. Perhaps you can spot cars moving on US-285, as it crosses Kenosha Pass into South Park.

Overleaf: A golden sunset casts its magic spell on Mount Bierstadt as seen from the Mount Evans Wilderness Area.

Windswept alpine tundra provides a year-around food source for mountain goats commonly seen along the upper portions of Stevens Gulch, as Grays and Torreys define the crest of America's Continental Divide.

Stevens Gulch ●

One of the most popular climbs in Colorado. Expect plenty of company for this easy trail hike for one or two fourteeners. A special attraction is the high probability of seeing mountain goats along the trail.

Chihuahua Gulch ●

A seldom used, off-trail, equally easy alternative to the busy eastern approach. Begins on the west side of the divide and follows another old mine road.

Horseshoe Basin (Grays) ●

Easy off-trail talus for one summit with few fellow climbers. The high mountains surrounding the basin provide a distinct alpine character.

Grizzly Gulch (Torreys) ■

A moderately difficult northeast approach which skirts the scenic face as seen from I-70. Off-trail with some bushwhacking required.

Grays Peak

14,270

From the Top: The top of the Continental Divide in America makes for an unbroken panorama of mountains. To the southwest are several ski areas; Keystone and Breckenridge are most easily spotted. South of Breckenridge is the fluted north slope of Quandary. From Quandary the nearby triple of Lincoln, Democrat and Bross should be evident.

Torreys Peak

14,267

From the Top: To the north and down 4000 feet is I-70 and the Bakerville Bridge. With binoculars you can see cars on US-6 as it winds up to Loveland Pass. Holy Cross is visible on the western horizon.

A blue-green water hole in the frozen ice of Chihuahua Lake with Torreys and Grays peaks looming beyond.

Reddish sandstone buttresses of the Garden of the Gods frame Pikes Peak.

Pikes Peak

14,110

From the Top: It is possible to see Pikes Peak from the Colorado–Wyoming border 150 miles to the north, and the view from the summit seems limitless. To the west the high summits of the Sangre de Cristo and Sawatch Ranges can be identified by the practiced eye. Take a map and see how many you can locate.

Barr Trail ●

Colorado's finest fourteener trail eases a long hike. The trail traverses four distinct vegetation zones: Foothills, Montane, Subalpine, and Alpine.

Summit Descents ●

A possibility with Pikes is to drive to the summit and then descend and climb back to your vehicle. Both the Barr Trail and the south slope to the reservoirs below are excellent choices. How far you descend is left to your climbing ethic.

Pikes Peak as seen from the high ridge of the Rampart Range.

Ten Mile and Mosquito Ranges

Ten Mile Range

Geologically the Ten Mile and Mosquito Ranges are part of the same uplift. The Continental Divide which bisects them defines their connecting line. They share a rich mining history from the turn of the century. Today the Ten Mile Range is a recreation mecca with one of the country's largest ski areas and the immensely popular Breckenridge to Vail bicycle trail wrapping around the base of the range. While having but one fourteener, the range boasts a half dozen of Colorado's highest hundred summits, the Century Peaks.

Somewhat less glamorous is the Climax Mine which straddles the Continental Divide on the west side of the range. Bartlett Mountain has already given of its summit to quench a modern world's thirst for molybdenum. This metal is an important alloying agent for steel. We covet a chrome-moly bicycle frame for its strength and toughness; chances are the moly came from this mine.

In place of the historic extractive industries, the communities at the base of the Ten Mile Range are turning increasingly to recreation. Alpine skiing is by far the dominant form of recreation in Summit County. Three of the range's numbered summits are used by the Breckenridge Ski Area, those being Peaks 8, 9 and 10. Current plans call for a funicular, a cable-driven surface lift, to be built to the summit of Peak 8, 12,987 feet.

Nordic skiing is also very popular and a possible means of climbing nearby summits. If you are seeking mountain solitude instead of high speed thrills, the range offers many trails. These trails will satisfy all skill levels from beginner to expert.

Mosquito Range

Mining, mining, mining describes the Mosquito Range. To the very tops of its four fourteeners you will find ample evidence of this activity. Roads, buildings and shafts occur at all levels up to and above 14,000 feet. The combination of the rounded nature of these peaks and the extensive road system make these the easiest fourteeners in the state. Most people do the triple of Lincoln, Democrat and Bross in one easy day. Old buildings, aerial trams, even funiculars are still in evidence in and around these summits. Colorado's largest gold nuggets came from Pennsylvania Mountain, between Bross and Sherman. The most recent nugget came out of the ground in 1989. Maybe you can spot such a precious find as you hike the high peaks.

Equally precious is the water that these summits hold for a parched plains population. Mount Democrat is the start for two of Colorado's major rivers. Its western slope is the beginning of the Arkansas River, while to the north is the South Platte River.

The mountain bike is perhaps the favorite vehicle of the recreational enthusiasts. In addition to many trails, there are 4WD roads, railroad grades and the possibility of three fourteeners. Lincoln, Bross and Sherman all have extensive 4WD road systems to tempt skilled bike riders.

Summit	Elevation	Rank	Page
Quandary Peak	14,265	12	25
Mount Lincoln	14,286	8	27
Mount Bross	14,172	22	27
Mount Democrat	14,148	29	27
Mount Sherman	14,036	45	29

Buckskin Creek washes over the varied gravel which once was part of the snowcapped Mount Democrat.

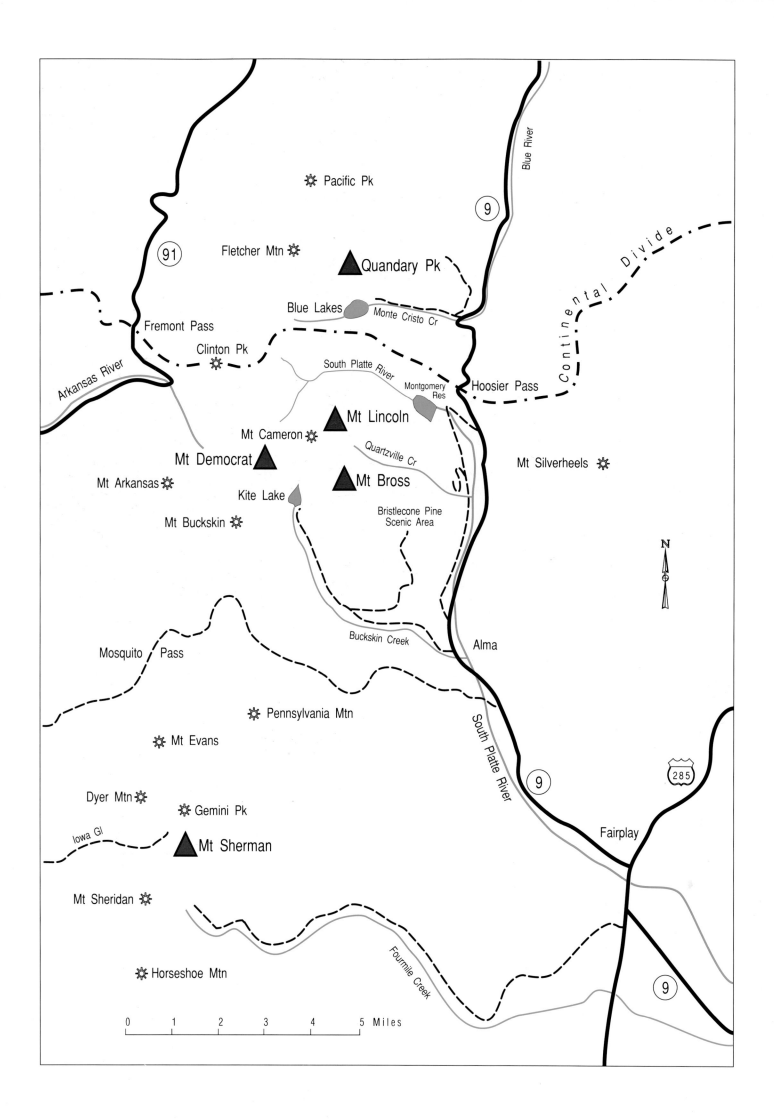

One of the numerous mine structures surrounding Quandary Peak.

Monte Cristo Creek ●

Easy flower-covered lower slopes lead to a firm talus trail. This is a popular winter ski route for the experienced mountaineer.

Blue Lakes ■

Starting from the dam, a 3000 foot direct route leads up the steep south side. This steep grunt saves a few hundred feet.

Quandary Peak

14,265

From the Top: The northern summits of the Sawatch Range from La Plata to Holy Cross form a western arc. South Park can be viewed looking over Hoosier Pass. Many mines dot the slopes of North Star Mountain, slightly more than a mile south. See if you can follow the imaginary line of the Continental Divide as it goes from Hoosier Pass, then west over North Star Mountain to Fremont and Tennessee Passes before disappearing between Massive and Holy Cross.

Just below the summit of Lincoln a lonesome mine bunkhouse overlooks Quartzville Creek and Mount Bross.

Kite Lake ●

The classic three-fourteeners-in-one-day climb. One, two or three summits are available if you start with Democrat and follow the ridge of the high alpine cirque.

Quartzville Creek (Lincoln) ●

An old 4WD road leads to a summit surrounded by many mines and buildings. The road which used to connect to Bross is an easy hike.

Windy Ridge (Bross) ●

If you don't mind a steep descent into Quartzville creek, this trail offers a potential circle route. Also, a long but gentle winter ski route for a fourteener.

Mount Lincoln from the south flanks of North Star Mountain. Look down the frosty wooden ore chute and imagine yourself being a miner ninety years ago dumping your cart of precious rock.

Mount Lincoln

14,286

From the Top: Colorado's eighth highest summit has mine structures encircling its high top. Most of them are but flattened kindling piles today, nonetheless a testament to the determination of our forefathers. Many distant summits are visible and with careful attention naming them will not be too difficult from this oxygen-starved pinnacle.

Mount Bross

14,172

From the Top: Bross has the best view of the immense South Park. Sherman is but eight miles south and still it is hard to locate due to several Century summits surrounding its flanks.

Mount Democrat

14,148

From the Top: The extensive Climax Mine just below and north of Democrat is a sobering realization of our demand for metal and the price the earth must pay. Easily the largest surface mine in Colorado, it has already consumed one mountain summit. The tailings from this mine have long since devoured the town of Kokomo, north of Fremont Pass.

Mount Sherman basks in the alpenglow as seen from Iowa Gulch.

Fourmile Creek ●

An easy road and trail to the ridge, then a long fun ridge walk. Old mines surround the route to add interest to the barren landscape.

Iowa Gulch ●

The seldom climbed western approach offers a circle route and two nearby Century peaks. This path crosses a stream and willow-covered valley.

Mosquito Pass ■

A 13,000+ foot off-trail route going up and down gentle ridges with one short, difficult, exposed ridge. The whole trip is less than two hours.

Mount Sherman

14,036

From the Top: Like its northern brothers, Sherman has old mines all around. The southeast side has the Dauntless and Hilltop mines. To the west is the Continental Chief directly below the summit. Further west are Leadville, Turquoise Reservoir and Mount Massive.

The weathered-wood of the Hill Top Mine acts as a native frame for the soft contours of Mount Sherman.

Sangre de Cristo and Culebra Ranges

Sangre de Cristo Range

The Sangre de Cristos formed the eastern boundary of Colorado's earliest white settlements. Most of the land was part of huge Spanish land grants dating to the early 1800's. The mix of Spanish and Anglo names for the mountains in this range reflect the area's human history.

The Spanish called the range Sangre de Cristo, or blood of Christ, likely referencing the frequent blood red sunsets. The names on the eastern side are mostly Anglo, due to much later settlement by Anglo ranchers and miners.

The fourteeners in the range are clustered into two groups: the Crestones, and the Sierra Blanca. The Crestones in particular are an awe inspiring group of conglomerate mountains. Conglomerate rock is rounded river boulders which have been re-cemented together and upthrust in a second mountain building phase. To witness the multicolored rounded forms in a matrix of red metamorphic sandstone is a humbling experience. To man, mountains are forever, and this scene is a vision of twice forever; an incomprehensible time span which forces the viewer to reflect and wonder.

Further south is the Sierra Blanca, Spanish for white mountains. While slightly less steep than the Crestones, they still offer a formidable climbing challenge. Little Bear in this group makes my select list of the hardest five. The approach to Lake Como is the most memorable part of these summits, particularly if you 4WD to the lake. The east side affords the most scenic views of Blanca and Ellingwood, but these beautiful steep faces are seldom climbed. The entire southern slopes of this group are on private land and part of the massive Forbes Ranch properties.

Culebra Range

Culebra is a Spanish word meaning snake. The range is generally considered part of the Sangre de Cristo Range. Culebra Peak is the only fourteener and it is entirely on private land. The west side of Culebra Peak is part of the Taylor Ranch; the east side is also private and off limits. As fourteeners go, Culebra is an easy climb but it offers relatively uninteresting scenery.

Summit	Elevation	Rank	Page
Humboldt Peak	14,064	37	33
Kit Carson Mountain	14,165	23	33
Crestone Peak	14,294	7	37
Crestone Needle	14,197	18	37
Mount Lindsey	14,042	42	39
Ellingwood Point	14,042	42	41
Blanca Peak	14,345	4	41
Little Bear Peak	14,037	44	41
Culebra Peak	14,047	41	43

Kit Carson Mountain as seen from the 14,000 foot red saddle between the twin summits of Crestone Peak.

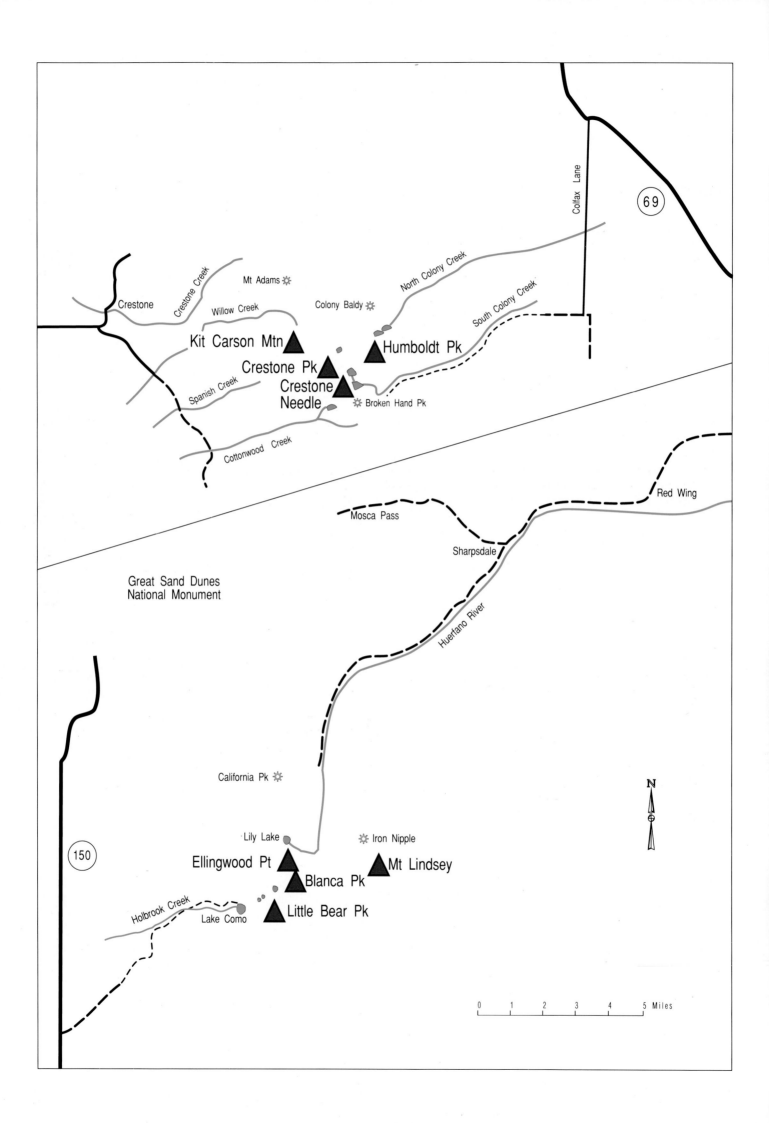

Crestone Creek

Crestone

Mt Adams ☀

Willow Creek

Colony Baldy ☀

North Colony Creek

South Colony Creek

Colfax Lane

69

Kit Carson Mtn ▲

Crestone Pk ▲

Crestone Needle ▲

☀ Broken Hand Pk

Humboldt Pk ▲

Spanish Creek

Cottonwood Creek

Red Wing

Mosca Pass

Sharpsdale

Great Sand Dunes
National Monument

Huerfano River

California Pk ☀

Lily Lake

☀ Iron Nipple

150

Ellingwood Pt ▲

Blanca Pk ▲

Mt Lindsey ▲

Holbrook Creek

Lake Como

Little Bear Pk ▲

N

0 1 2 3 4 5 Miles

Just below Lower South Colony Lake these delightful tarns provide a tranquil view of Humboldt Peak.

South Colony Lakes (Humboldt) ■

A long rough 4WD road, followed by an easy trail into one of Colorado's premier alpine basins. The steep grunt to the saddle is rewarded by magnificent views of the Crestones, then a moderate ridge walk to the summit.

South Colony Lakes (Kit Carson) ♦♦

A panoramic ridge walk leads to the Bears Playground followed by a steep ascent of the east summit. The famed and feared steep descent off the east summit earns Kit Carson its very difficult status.

Spanish Creek (Kit Carson) ♦

Less traveled, and less difficult than the more popular route above. The approach is from Crestone on the west side of the range.

Humboldt Peak

14,064

From the Top: East of Humboldt is the broad Wet Mountain Valley with the twin towns of Westcliffe and Silver Cliff as its economic hub. Far more imposing are the eastern faces of Crestone Needle and Crestone Peak as they rise precipitously out of South Colony Valley. North of the Crestones is the Bears Playground and Kit Carson Mountain.

Kit Carson Mountain

14,165

From the Top: To the north is the steep north face of Kit Carson with the grassy expanse of Willow Creek beyond. South is the north face of Crestone Peak with the continuation of the red gully and its distinct cliff as the gully bends west. The hundred-mile-long San Luis Valley dominates the western view with the distant San Juans on the horizon.

Overleaf: The view of the Crestones, The Bears Playground, and Kit Carson from Humboldt's summit.

Crestone Needle and Crestone Peak as seen from the north side of the Bears Playground.

South Colony Lakes ◆◆

A beautiful high alpine basin is the beginning for two difficult summits. The sturdy conglomerate rock makes for secure albeit steep climbing. Expect lots of people at the lakes due to the access provided by the 4WD road.

Cottonwood Lake ◆

Easier than South Colony, and the route of choice if a backpack is required. The trail to Cottonwood Lake is moderate with few to no people on the west side.

Crestone Peak

14,294

From the Top: Kit Carson to the north looks like a faceted jewel with its many glacier-carved ridges. Southward along the western foothills of the Sangre de Cristo are the immense sand dunes of Sand Dunes National Monument. Just beyond is the Sierra Blanca with its four fourteeners.

Crestone Needle

14,197

From the Top: The small summit looks directly down onto Colony Lakes, 2500 feet below. To the northwest are the summits of Crestone and Kit Carson. Notice the steep ridge connecting the two Crestones. Pikes Peak can be seen on the northeast horizon.

Crestone Needle from Upper South Colony Lake with a seemingly floating island of flowers.

Mount Lindsey as seen from the summit of Blanca, the highest point in the Sangre de Cristo.

Fun 4 Factor

Huerfano Basin ■

A combined trail and off-trail hike with some steep areas on the north summit ridge. Study the route closely because the summit will not be visible until almost 13,000 feet.

Mount Lindsey

14,042

From the Top: Eastward is La Veta Pass with the impressive bulk of West Spanish Peak, 13,626 feet, slightly south. From the pass and south of the summit in a large sweep are the Forbes Ranch properties. Lindsey's summit is on private land. To the west is Blanca and a number of high alpine basins with inviting lakes. An unnamed Century summit is less than a mile northeast of the Iron Nipple.

Blanca and Ellingwood define the beginning of the Huerfano River. Scenes such as this enrich your climb of Lindsey.

The infamous Blanca–Little Bear ridge as seen from the summit of Blanca Peak. Lake Como is to the right.

Lake Como (Blanca and Ellingwood) ■

One of Colorado's toughest 4WD roads leads to and past Lake Como. Then a rocky trail hike past numerous alpine lakes leads to the ridge saddle, followed by moderate ridge walks to each summit.

Lake Como (Little Bear) ♦♦

A steep, loose gully advances to a fun ridge walk, followed by the very steep and solid summit gully. Finally, a series of gravel-covered benches end at the small summit.

This section of steep rock gives Little Bear its 'very difficult' ranking. Most people free climb up and rappel down. Look for fixed anchors above the climbers.

Ellingwood Point

14,042

From the Top: The north face of Blanca dominates the southern horizon. Slightly west is Little Bear with the connecting ridge between them. Northeast is the Huerfano River Basin with Lily Lake just below the summit. Lake Como can be seen at the edge of the trees to the west.

Blanca Peak

14,345

From the Top: Located at the corner of three counties, Huerfano, Costilla, and Alamosa, you have a measure of the importance of this summit. To the south, west and north lies a patchwork quilt of farms in the vast San Luis Valley. Closer, you can look down on the famed Blanca–Little Bear Ridge. To the north are the Crestones with numerous summits in between.

Little Bear Peak

14,037

From the Top: A series of steep ridges emanate from Little Bear's summit. As they disappear the next thing one sees is the agricultural patchwork miles below. The ridge to the east connects to Blanca and is very rugged.

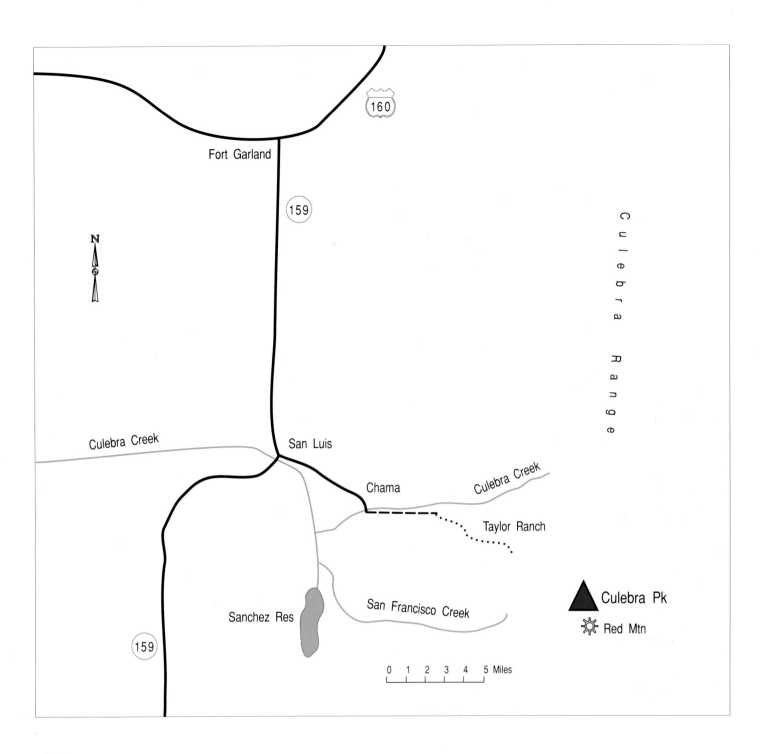

Taylor Ranch ●

Colorado's only pay fourteener, consequently climbed only by those interested in a Colorado Grand Slam. Easy terrain to hike and if the ranch allows use of its 4WD road, the route is that much shorter.

Culebra Peak

14,047

From the Top: The view west is blocked by the high west ridge. Northeast are the twin summits of the Spanish Peaks. Below and east is the small locale of Torres. To the south is a Century peak, Red Mountain, 13,908 feet.

When Culebra was open to climbing any Sunday in July, large crowds gathered on the summit. Chances are 90 percent of the people up there are near the end of their Grand Slam.

Sawatch Range

As the table shows, the Sawatch Range has almost one-third of Colorado's fourteen thousand foot peaks and its three highest summits. Those three are within fifteen feet of the same elevation. Interestingly, even though the Continental Divide runs along the range for seventy miles, it never crosses one of these high summits. Also, only Holy Cross is on the western side of the divide.

An important sub-group of summits are the Collegiate Peaks which are summits named after important colleges of the late 1800's. The five Collegiate Peaks are: Columbia, Harvard, Princeton, Oxford and Yale.

As a north-south range, most of the drainages go east-west to empty into the headwaters of one of America's major rivers, the Arkansas. The biggest of these drainages headwater on the eastern slopes of the Continental Divide and flow east to the Arkansas River. The Arkansas headwaters along the west slopes of Mount Democrat in the Mosquito Range starting above 12,000 feet and exits past Salida at less than 7000 feet. This seventy-mile stretch of water is considered the Upper Arkansas River. The major Sawatch creeks which feed the Arkansas are: Halfmoon, Lake, Clear, Pine, Cottonwood, Chalk, and Poncha. Additionally the South Fork of the Arkansas River drains the Monarch Pass region. Most of these streams have some form of a road following their courses. These vary from a modern paved two-lane highway to narrow rutted 4WD roads.

Colorado's big game mammals abound throughout the range with the newest addition, the non-native mountain goat, doing particularly well. Elk, mule deer, and bighorn sheep also flourish at varying elevations. For the climber of fourteeners it is the white mountain goat which is most easily viewed. This is due to its easy-to-see color, and its relative lack of fear of man. The other species were almost wiped out early in the twentieth century by meat hunters. At this juncture in the twentieth century most of the animals are at record high numbers due to a fee-based sport hunting program which generates significant monies for habitat improvement and hunting regulation.

Summit	Elevation	Rank	Page
Mount of the Holy Cross	14,005	52	47
Mount Massive	14,421	2	49
Mount Elbert	14,433	1	51
La Plata Peak	14,336	5	53
Mount Oxford	14,153	27	57
Mount Belford	14,197	18	57
Missouri Mountain	14,067	36	57
Huron Peak	14,005	52	59
Mount Harvard	14,420	3	63
Mount Columbia	14,073	35	63
Mount Yale	14,196	21	65
Mount Princeton	14,197	18	67
Mount Antero	14,269	10	71
Mount Shavano	14,229	17	73
Mount Tabeguache	14,155	26	73

Mount Elbert, Colorado's highest summit, is reflected off of Crystal Lake.

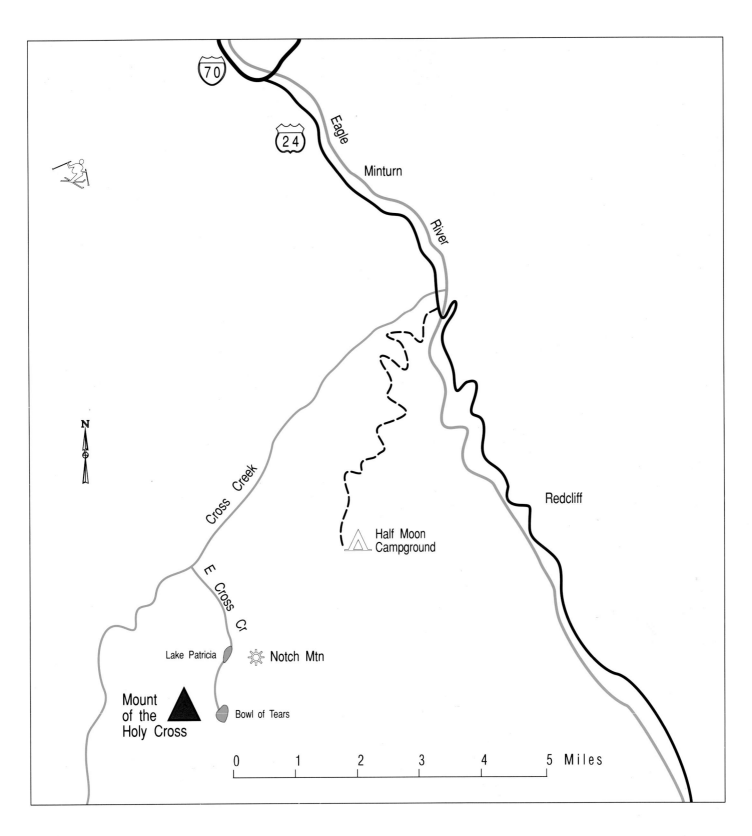

The map shows the area with the following labels: I-70, US-24, Eagle River, Minturn, Redcliff, Cross Creek, E Cross Cr, Half Moon Campground, Lake Patricia, Notch Mtn, Mount of the Holy Cross, Bowl of Tears.

N

0   1   2   3   4   5 Miles

Fun **6** Factor

Half Moon Pass ▪

Long and beautiful, with lots of Columbine in July. The trail is very good to East Cross Creek and only slightly less so to and past timberline.

Shortly after crossing Half Moon Pass this beautiful panorama of Mount of the Holy Cross welcomes the hiker.

Notch Top Mountain provides this view of Holy Cross' namesake snowfield in June.

Mount of the Holy Cross

14,005

From the Top: The view from the top is one of geologically recent glaciation. Steeply sculpted U–shaped valleys with bare rock walls make it unlike any other Sawatch fourteener. Looking south the monarchs of the Sawatch, Elbert and Massive are quickly spotted. Torreys and Grays on the divide far to the east are easy to identify.

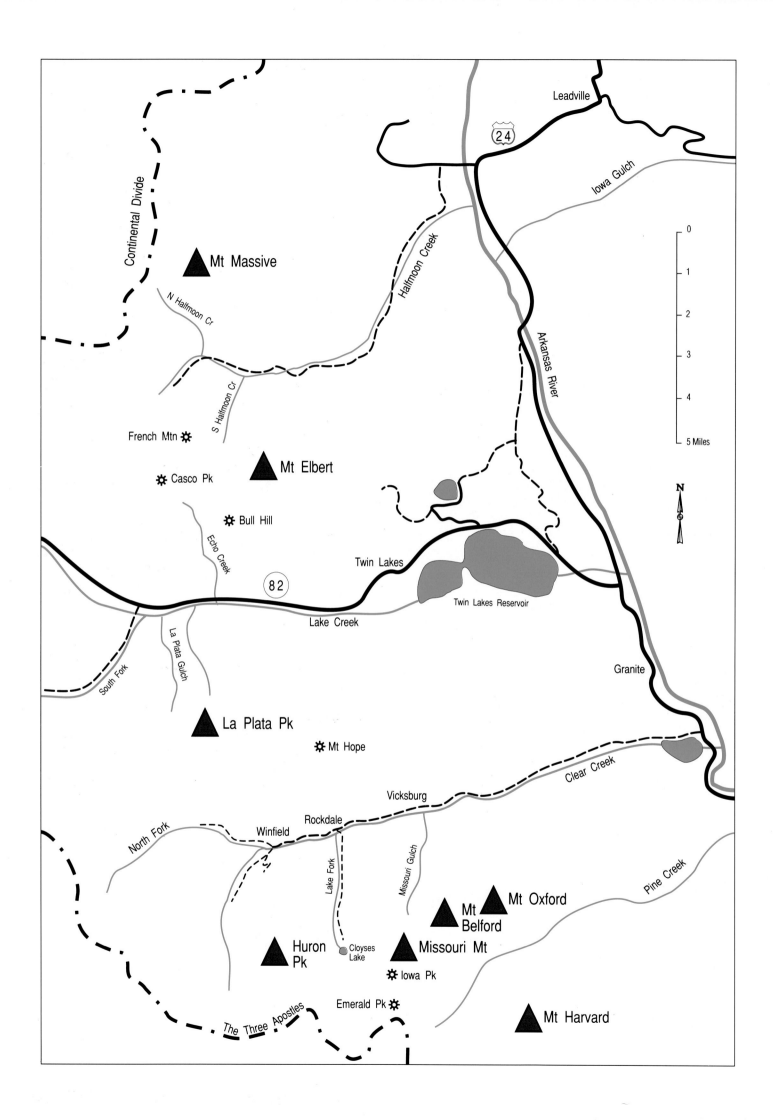

A tarn along North Halfmoon Creek provides this foreground view of Mount Massive's ridge summit.

Colorado Trail ⬤

A great trail to timberline, then slightly steeper to the ridge saddle, followed by a fun ridge walk. Lots of flowers in July to treat the eye.

North Halfmoon Creek ◼

A western approach which is shorter and steeper than the heavily traveled Colorado Trail. The photo above gives a good indication of the terrain.

Mount Massive

14,421

From the Top: The most distinctive view from Massive is not even in the Sawatch Range, but rather in the nearby Elk Mountains. Mount Sopris, not even 13,000 feet, stands as a lone sentinel at the northwest corner of the Elks. The reason such a relatively low mountain stands out is its almost 7000 feet of relief compared to the nearby Crystal River Valley. To the east Leadville commands the high ground of the broad upper Arkansas Valley.

A morning mist on one of the Mount Massive Lakes reflect a somber Mount Elbert.

Colorado Trail ●

A trail hike to timberline followed by a long walk up a broad ridge. Because this is the easiest route on Colorado's highest summit, expect plenty of company.

South Halfmoon Creek ■

Depending on where you park your vehicle, the route length varies. The part past timberline is the steeper of these four choices.

Mount Elbert Trail ●

Similar to the Colorado Trail in summer. Finding the trailhead is the only additional difficulty. The best choice for a winter ascent.

Bull Hill ■

Starts off of CO-82 and approaches from the south. An altitude junkie's delight for the hours spent above timberline.

Mount Elbert

14,433

From the Top: A 360 degree panorama of fourteeners can be seen from Colorado's highest. North are Massive and Holy Cross, east is Sherman, south are all the summits of the Sawatch, and west is Snowmass with its expansive namesake snowfield still visible in early summer.

The semi-frozen surface of Turquoise Lake in May with a distant Mount Elbert. One week later the lake was ice-free.

La Plata Peak as seen from the northwest. Ellingwood Ridge is partially obscured by the twin spruce trees.

South Fork ■

The north ridge standard route, neither hard nor easy. Crossing the South Fork of Lake Creek is the major difficulty. Nice views after timberline of the north face and Ellingwood Ridge.

Winfield ●

The finest climb in the Sawatch (see photo page 59). Mostly off-trail through a high mountain meadow, followed by a short steep gully, then a wide ridge leading to the summit.

La Plata Peak

14,336

From the Top: On the western horizon five of the Elk fourteeners can be identified: from left to right look for Castle, Maroon, Pyramid, Snowmass and Capitol. Closer on the Continental Divide, between Pyramid and Snowmass, is Grizzly Peak, 13,988 feet, thought to be a fourteener until a re-survey in the late 1940's.

From high on the south-facing slopes of Bull Hill, La Plata Peak looms over the rugged Ellingwood Ridge.

Overleaf: Four fourteeners in a row—Oxford, Belford, Missouri and Huron—seen from immediately north of Clear Creek and east of Vicksburg.

Minutes after a September snow squall the sun blankets upper Missouri Gulch and Missouri Mountain.

Vicksburg ■

Moderate in length, but easy on and off-trail for two or three summits. The north face of Missouri is noticeably more difficult. Good camping in the basin.

Cloyses Lake (Missouri) ●

Easier for Missouri than the Missouri Gulch route, also makes for easy access to two Century peaks: Iowa and Emerald.

Mount Oxford

14,153

From the Top: Look north to pick out US-24 in the wide, flat upper Arkansas Valley. Above the road on the horizon is Holy Cross. To the south is Harvard with the distant Mount Princeton to the left.

Mount Belford

14,197

From the Top: The rounded top of Belford offers little opportunity to examine lower features. All of the Mosquito fourteeners are within a five degree arc to the northeast.

Missouri Mountain

14,067

From the Top: Many near and far summits can be identified from the steep summit of Missouri. Massive is directly behind Elbert and therefore obscured. Missouri Gulch lays like an open book to the north.

Mounts Oxford and Belford seen through the weathered wooden window frame of the Columbine Mine cabin.

Huron Peak and The Three Apostles, taken from the unnamed basin which is the southern approach to La Plata.

Winfield ●

Two easy off-trail variations with a possibility of one for the ascent and the other for the descent. Great views of the nearby Three Apostles.

Cloyses Lake ■

An off-trail and slightly steeper route which puts you on the saddle between Browns and Huron. Excellent camping possibilities along Lake Fork of Clear Creek.

Huron Peak

14,005

From the Top: Even though ranked 52nd in height, Huron provides one of the best viewing summits in the Sawatch. The summit is very small with steep sides so the near view is excellent and its relative position allows for extended peak picking. My favorite is Uncompahgre eighty-plus miles to the southwest, which is characterized by its black block summit.

Overleaf: The lush-green Mount Columbia looking across Frenchman Creek.

A grass-lined tarn on Harrison Flats reflects Huron Peak in late August.

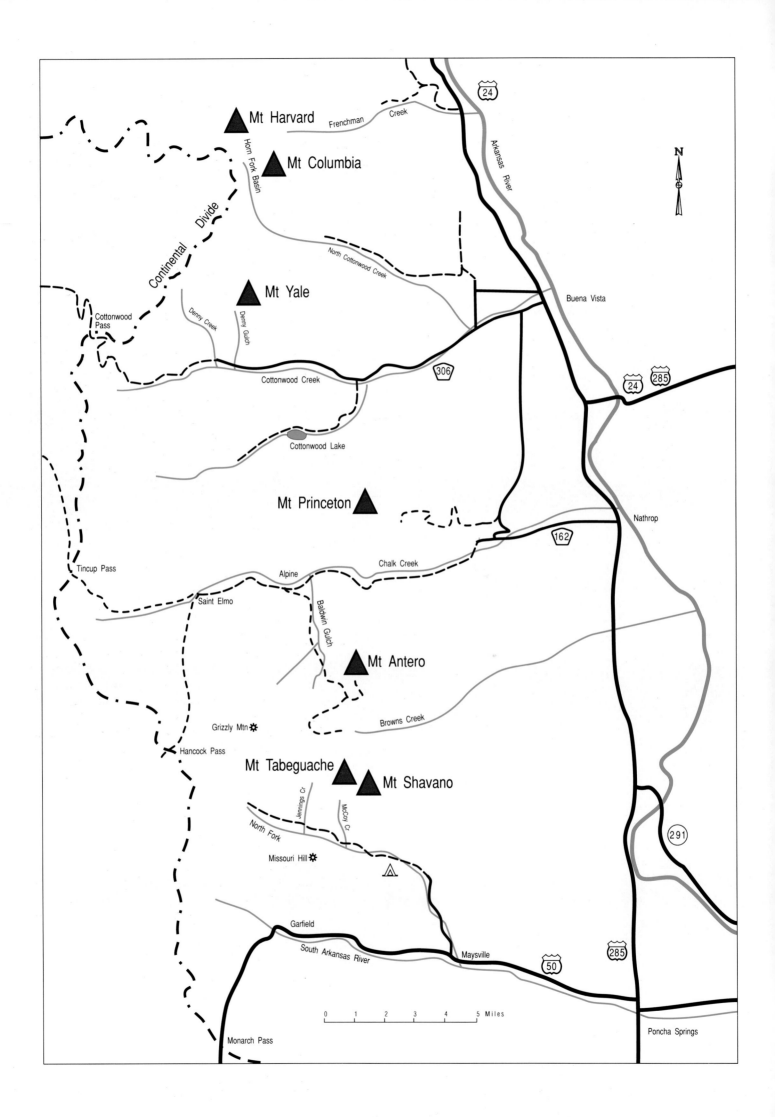

A 13,000 foot high alpine tarn reflects Mount Harvard at sunrise.

Horn Fork Basin ■

A long day hike for one or two summits, but better as a camping trip into a heavily used valley. Columbia by itself is steep and loose.

Frenchman Creek / Harvard Trail ●

A little used, beautiful alternative to the more popular Horn Fork trail. Excellent camping at or below timberline. Allows for two separate climbs and avoids the difficult connecting ridge.

Mount Harvard

14,420

From the Top: Look east over the much lower Mosquito Range ridge and see most of South Park, with Pikes Peak clearly visible beyond. Southward you can see a half dozen more Sawatch summits. Southwest are the San Juans with several identifiable peaks. West are the Elks with Castle closest and Capitol most distant. North are another half dozen Sawatch summits. The large lake to the west is Taylor Park Reservoir.

Mount Columbia

14,073

From the Top: Harvard at the head of Horn Fork Basin will dominate the view from Columbia. Otherwise the Arkansas River valley from Leadville to Salida is visible. Take time to enjoy the serpentine sweep of the Continental Divide, just across Horn Fork Basin.

Holywater Beaver Ponds provide this dramatic reflection of Mount Yale and its south false summit.

Denny Gulch ●

An easy summer hike with a loose scree field as the biggest obstacle. In winter a physically demanding adventure.

Mount Yale

14,196

From the Top: Yale has the best view of Horn Fork Basin with Harvard at the end and Columbia defining the eastern boundary. The Elks to the northwest line up in an almost straight line. The south boundary of the Collegiate Peaks Wilderness Area below roughly follows the Cottonwood Pass Road.

A foothills beaver pond on Sevenmile Creek with the snow-covered Mount Yale in the distance.

The previous night's snow and magic sunlight drape Mount Princeton and the South Sawatch summits.

Frontier Ranch ●

An easy road and trail hike, or if a 4WD is used, an easier trail-only hike. Good chance of seeing mountain goats above timberline.

Alternate routes ■

Cascade Canyon and Cottonwood Lake are alternatives to the busy eastern approach. Both involve some bushwhacking below timberline and considerably more elevation gain. Cascade Canyon is a southern route from Alpine at 8800 feet. Cottonwood Lake is at 9600 feet and is northwest of the summit.

Mount Princeton

14,197

From the Top: Because Princeton juts east from the body of the Sawatch Range, the Arkansas and Trout Creek valleys are easily viewed. Two trains once crossed Trout Creek Pass into the Arkansas Valley. One train headed north to Leadville and the other went up Chalk Creek past Saint Elmo and through the Alpine Tunnel. Both of these railroad beds can be spotted by the keen-eyed observer.

Gnarled aspen boles frame Mount Princeton as seen from the Goddard Ranch homestead.

Overleaf: A tranquil early-October scene of golden cottonwoods, a boiling Arkansas River, and snow-covered Mount Princeton.

Morning alpenglow illuminates a bristlecone pine remnant and Mount Antero, as seen from Bristlecone Park on Mount Princeton's southeast slopes.

Baldwin Gulch ●

A popular 4WD road is the primary route for most of this hike. Because the road is so rough, dust is not a major problem. Consider a June climb if you wish to avoid the vehicles.

Mount Antero

14,269

From the Top: If the air is clear the view south over Poncha Pass shows the west side of the Sangre de Cristos as far south as the Sierra Blanca. The sand dunes are easily spotted below the Sierra Blanca. This view is best when the sun is low in the west.

Mount Antero as seen from Granite Mountain to the northwest.

The warm glow of sunrise bathes an alpine tarn with the reflected glow of Mounts Shavano and Tabeguache.

This view of Tabeguache and Shavano from Missouri Hill shows both Jennings and McCoy Creeks.

Angel of Shavano / Colorado Trail ●
More elevation gain than Jennings Creek but easier climbing. Early in the year a glissade on the Angel is a possibility.

McCoy Creek ◆
The shortest and most difficult choice for these summits. Good camping at timberline if you don't mind 'vertical' backpacking.

Jennings Creek ■
The most popular route is still long and strenuous. The early part is steep, loose scree with solid ridges for the remainder. It requires the re-climbing of Tabeguache to descend.

Browns Creek ●
If you can get to Browns Creek at timberline, potentially the easiest route for these two summits, and also it is the least crowded.

Mount Shavano
14,229
From the Top: The Arkansas Valley widens considerably near Salida to the southeast and this is the commanding vantage point. Pikes Peak is a little north of east on the horizon. The San Luis Valley opens up to the south.

Mount Tabeguache
14,155
From the Top: Seven miles southwest is Monarch Pass with the antennas visible on the Continental Divide ridge and US-50 winding up the grade. Parts of Monarch Ski Area are visible. To the north the road system on the south side of Antero scars the landscape.

Elk Mountains

This is the most scenic and difficult to climb range in the state with a tremendous contrast in rock types. Castle to the east is metamorphic, similar to the nearby Sawatch. Pyramid and the Bells are metamorphic sedimentary mudstone. The two western fourteeners are plutonic, as one giant intrusive batholith. The major summits of Yosemite are plutonic in origin. This homogeneous rock forms when one tectonic plate is thrust over another plate. The rock of the lower plate is superheated and flows upward like an upside-down droplet of water into the top plate. This droplet either vents as a volcano or cools into a homogenous mass, which then is exposed by subsequent glaciation. Mount Sopris, further west, is this same rock type. All around Snowmass and Capitol are sedimentary mudstone mountains of various colors.

The mineral-rich rock supports a rich flora that delights the eye. Aspen and scrub oak dominate the lower elevations, with spruce to treeline and lush flowers in the alpine zone. These flowers grow even on the summits of the fourteeners, particularly the sedimentary summits. This is a tribute to both the richness of the soil and the hardiness of these plants.

Climbing the Elks is characterized by long approaches and steep ascents. None is easy and most are difficult or harder. The reward for your effort is awesome views and complete lack of boredom. All can be climbed from the Aspen side of the range with only Snowmass accessible from the south.

Plan your trip to these summits to avoid the monsoon rains with their accompanying lightning. This strategy will give you the most flexibility and lessen the climbing danger.

Summit	Elevation	Rank	Page
Castle Peak	14,265	12	77
Pyramid Peak	14,018	47	81
North Maroon Peak	14,014	50	81
Maroon Peak	14,156	25	81
Capitol Peak	14,130	30	83
Snowmass Mountain	14,092	32	85

Pyramid Peak's east side from East Maroon Creek.

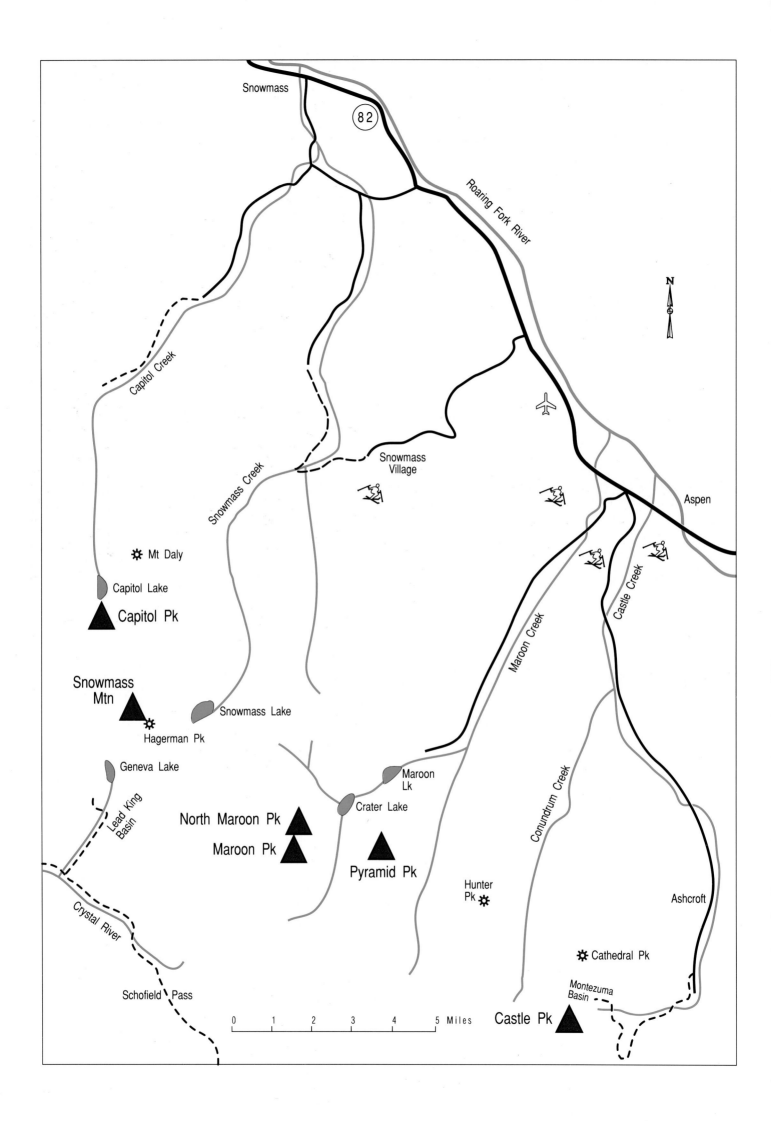

Along the Pearl Pass road, one of a series of rocky tarns reflects the southeast side of Castle Peak.

Fun 7 Factor

Ashcroft ◼

A delightful change of pace if you have only climbed Sawatch summits to date. Slightly harder with some exposure and top-of-the-world views . . . go for it!

Castle Peak

14,265

From the Top: If you climb Castle on the east ridge, just before reaching the height of the connecting saddle between Castle and Conundrum, the balance of the Elks will dramatically appear. Each of the fourteeners can be brought up close by a moderate telephoto lense. From left to right are Maroon, North Maroon, Snowmass, Capitol, and Pyramid. The gray-white monzonite of Snowmass and Capitol contrast with maroon formation rocks.

First Overleaf: The traditional view of the Maroon Bells, reflected in Maroon Lake, with swirling fog and clouds masking the surroundings.

Second Overleaf: The Geneva Lake trail in Lead King Basin provides this non-traditional view of the Bells.

The sunny, flower-covered east slopes of North Maroon Peak give the climber an idea of the steep terrain.

Pyramid ◆

Fun **8** Factor

One of Colorado's more difficult fourteeners, also as beautiful as they come. If you have yet to attempt one of this triple treat, Pyramid is a good warm-up. Expect steep, sometimes exposed climbing with weak, slippery rock. The summit is a great place for a nap after a long tense climb, as it is surprisingly large and flat.

The Bells ◆◆

Fun **8** Factor

Wow!!! Read the Pyramid summary and subtract the large flat summit and nap—no time. These are Colorado's most photographed mountains, and the climb, particularly North Maroon, is every bit as beautiful. North Maroon, although shorter, is more difficult than Maroon, often considered the most difficult fourteener. North Maroon gets my vote.

Pyramid Peak

14,018

From the Top: Surrounded by a sea of high mountains, the view depends on the time of day and hence the direction of the light. The steep east face of the Bells is worth studying particularly if you have yet to climb them. Looking further west over Buckskin Pass are Snowmass and Capitol. To the east is an unbroken string of fourteeners in the Sawatch. Identifying them is very difficult due to a lack of familiar landmarks.

North Maroon Peak

14,014

From the Top: Look northeast to Maroon Lake and imagine the first time you saw the Bells and wondered if anyone could ever climb such a steep mountain. With binoculars you can see hundreds of scurrying tourists; perhaps some of them have binoculars and are watching the crazy climbers on the summit.

Maroon Peak

14,156

From the Top: If you just did the traverse, you need no more views for this day. If not, then enjoy Fravert Basin to the southwest and the beautiful maroon and green patchwork as flora and rock create infinite patterns.

The last thousand feet of Pyramid Peak as seen from the east side.

The clouds, combined with the gray-white rock of the Capitol batholith, create this dramatic monochromatic scene of the Pierre Lakes Basin. The view is from high on Snowmass' west ridge.

Capitol Creek ♦♦

The most beautiful approach to a fourteener. A long trail with Capitol in view almost the entire way whets your appetite for the climb. Good rock compensates for the occasional exposed section on the summit ridge.

Capitol Peak

14,130

From the Top: Look north at your approach and remember your thoughts. Capitol Lake is just below, and when you were there you wanted to be on top. Now that you are on top, you wish to sit on the lake's serene shores. Looking a little left you see the twin summits of Mount Sopris with buckskin and red-colored mountains between. Glance over to Snowmass and the picturesque parabolic ridges which connect these summits. Below to the left is the rugged Pierre Lakes Basin with its many shimmering lakes.

Capitol's infamous Knife Edge with Diente, the Grand Slam Dog. Because I couldn't protect him on the edge, I called him back after a dozen feet and we crossed lower and to the left.

Buckskin Pass provides this vantage point for Snowmass Mountain and Lake.

Snowmass Lake ▪

A long, lush, heavily used trail leads to the lake, followed by a mostly off-trail snow or rock route to the summit. The snow can make for quite an oven in the morning.

Lead King Basin ◆

This little-known day trip for Snowmass combines a rough 4WD road, a fine trail to Geneva Lake, and a difficult off-trail rock ending.

Snowmass Mountain

14,092

From the Top: The small top is steep on both sides and provides excellent views of two valleys. Southwest is Geneva Lake more than 3000 feet below. Siberia Lake is up the same valley. The east side is dominated by the namesake snowfield, except in late summer when the gray-white monzonite is revealed. The Bells are only five miles away and all but unrecognizable because of the unfamiliar view. Notice how North Maroon appears as an insignificant bump on Maroon Peak's north ridge.

The west side of Snowmass Mountain near Siberia Lake.

San Juan Range and La Garita Mountains

San Juan Range

This is the largest range of mountains in southwest Colorado, and as such it lends its name to the entire southwest corner of the state. The San Juan mountain groups which contain fourteeners include La Garita, Needle, San Miguel and Sneffels. Other significant mountain groups are part of the greater San Juans. They include the Cimarrons, Grenadiers and La Platas.

All of the many roads in the area owe their existence to mining. When silver enjoyed direct coinage in the 1890s, the area was booming. Today few of the ore bodies are rich enough to justify the expense of mining, and very few active mines exist today. Recreation has replaced mining as the dominant driver of the local economy. Hiking, fishing, jeeping, snowmobiling and hunting each contribute their share. Lake City, located at the confluence of Henson Creek and the Lake Fork of the Gunnison River, is the supply hub. All of the fourteeners are accessed via roads paralleling these two streams.

If time permits between your climbs, much enjoyable exploring can be had, either on foot or by 4WD. The 4WD mountain passes in this region are legendary and often a destination in themselves. Names which come quickly to mind are Engineer, Cinnamon, Ophir, Stony, Imogene and Black Bear. The switchbacks of the Black Bear Road—as it drops into Telluride—will get your undivided attention. Many others exist, and combined they provide unparalleled access to the highest part of Colorado.

The entire region is of volcanic origin with much evidence of this beginning, even to the amateur observer. Just north of Lake City massive ancient lava flows are visible on both sides of the Lake Fork. These no doubt dammed the river to create a huge lake until the rock was cut away by the ceaseless river. Higher up the evidence is one of carpets of volcanic ash covered by verdant flowers and grasses.

La Garita Mountains

Whether approaching San Luis from the northeast or the west, you will be struck by the remoteness of these mountains. Also notable is the subtle way the average elevation increases. When you first drive into Big Meadow your internal computer tells you that the elevation must be 9–10,000 feet. But your eyes say it is much higher, especially as soft, rounded mountains to the south appear without any trees. Something about human thought is that we trust our instinct before our eyes. The treeless, softly contoured mountain just to the south of the meadow is 13,401 foot Baldy Chato. The hidden San Luis is less than four miles south of Baldy Chato's summit. Big Meadow is over 11,000 feet and the long steady climb in your vehicle was masked by the numerous curves through the undulating Gunnison National Forest.

The La Garita Mountains straddle the Continental Divide at the eastern extreme of the greater San Juans. Like the rest of the San Juans they are of volcanic origin, but unlike their western brothers these are much softer in appearance. The lush forest obscures your view of these summits and not surprisingly the best vantage is from the La Garita's highest summit, San Luis Peak.

The abundant and expansive high meadows support large herds of elk. The dense forest provides superb cover as protection from would-be hunters. The best way to enjoy the sight of a herd is to scan the meadow fringes as the light waxes and wanes. Be very quiet as elk have superb hearing and are easily spooked.

Summit	Elevation	Rank	Page
San Luis Peak	14,014	50	89
Uncompahgre Peak	14,309	6	93
Wetterhorn Peak	14,015	49	93
Redcloud Peak	14,034	46	95
Sunshine Peak	14,001	54	95
Handies Peak	14,048	40	97

A wilderness study area off of Wagner Gulch includes this beaver pond which reflects the snow-covered twin summits of Sunshine and Redcloud.

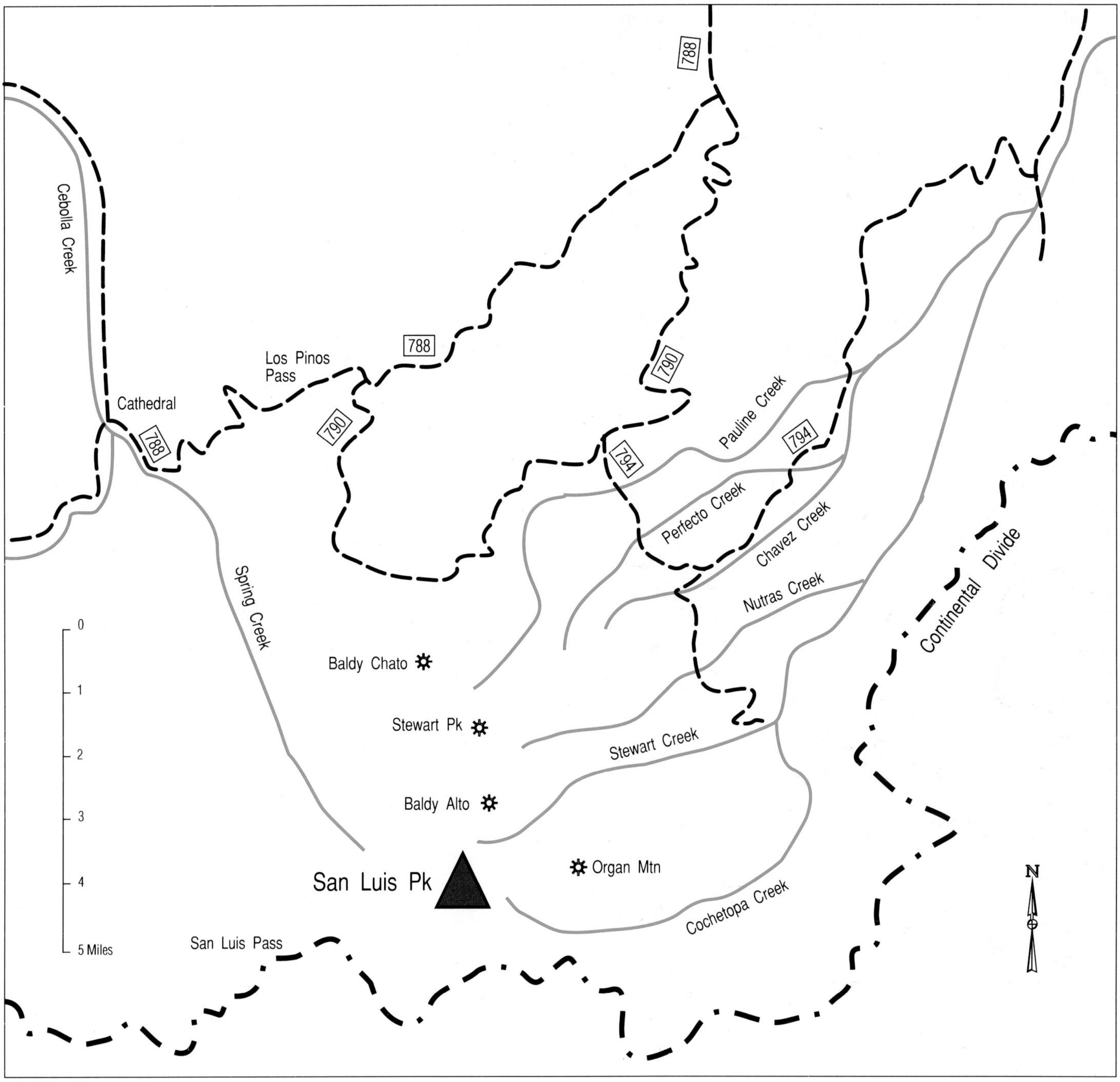

788
790
794
Cebolla Creek
Los Pinos Pass
Cathedral
Pauline Creek
Perfecto Creek
Chavez Creek
Nutras Creek
Spring Creek
Continental Divide
Baldy Chato
Stewart Pk
Stewart Creek
Baldy Alto
Organ Mtn
San Luis Pk
Cochetopa Creek
San Luis Pass
0
1
2
3
4
5 Miles
N

Fun 6 Factor

Stewart Creek ●

A good trail through lush timber followed by grassy slopes and a faint talus trail along the northeast ridge to San Luis.

San Luis Peak

14,014

From the Top: Creede, one of Colorado's legendary gold mining towns, is less than ten miles south, just across the Continental Divide. The divide is the soft ridge stretching east–west, less than two miles south of the summit. Due north is Gunnison, less than forty miles away. Uncompahgre Peak, thirty miles west, is always identifiable from any high southwestern summit.

First Overleaf: The ridge separating Big Blue and Nellie creeks provides this vantage of Uncompahgre Peak.

San Luis Peak as seen from San Luis Pass on the Continental Divide southwest of the summit.

Second Overleaf: Wetterhorn Peak as seen from the west fork of Matterhorn Creek.

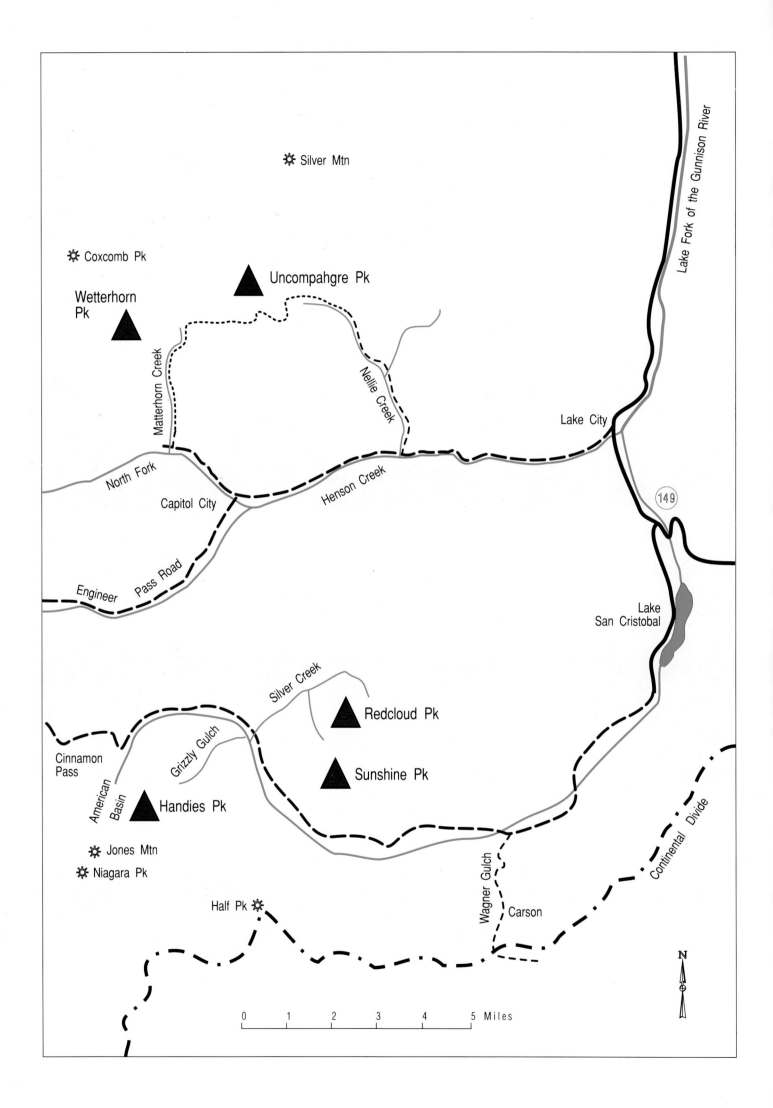

☼ Silver Mtn

☼ Coxcomb Pk

▲ Uncompahgre Pk

Wetterhorn
Pk ▲

Matterhorn Creek

Nellie Creek

Lake City

North Fork

Capitol City

Henson Creek

149

Engineer   Pass Road

Lake
San Cristobal

Silver Creek

▲ Redcloud Pk

Cinnamon
Pass

Grizzly Gulch

American Basin

▲ Sunshine Pk

▲ Handies Pk

☼ Jones Mtn

☼ Niagara Pk

Wagner Gulch

Carson

Continental Divide

Half Pk ☼

Lake Fork of the Gunnison River

N

0   1   2   3   4   5 Miles

A fresh snow blankets Uncompahgre Peak as seen above Nellie Creek.

Nellie Creek (Uncompahgre) ▪

Starting from the wilderness boundary trailhead, a short, spectacular hike to the highest summit in the San Juans. If starting from Henson Creek, subtract short.

Matterhorn Creek (Uncompahgre) ▪

A longer but easy route for Uncompahgre. This is the route of choice for those planning to climb both summits in one day.

Matterhorn Creek (Wetterhorn) ◆

Except for the last few hundred feet to the summit, a grassy, flower-covered slope hike. The final pitch is more difficult on the return because of the airy view.

Uncompahgre Peak

14,309

From the Top: The tallest summit in the greater San Juan region has a commanding view. Surprisingly it is not easy to identify fourteeners to the south. This is owing to the uncommon height of all the lesser peaks. To the west, Wetterhorn, Sneffels and the two Wilsons are easy marks. Hike north from the true summit a couple hundred feet for a great view of the northeast face looking down into Nellie Creek. The summit has ample flowers in July for your enjoyment.

Wetterhorn Peak

14,015

From the Top: Steep on all sides with a surprisingly large grassy summit from which the views are endless. Particularly interesting is the distinctive Cimarron Range to the west. A number of drainages have their headwaters around Wetterhorn. These same drainages often have hiking trails which can be seen from the summit.

A Burrows Park beaver pond provides a dramatic reflection of the west side of Redcloud and Sunshine.

Fun
3
Factor

Silver Creek ■

Redcloud and Sunshine are a pair of classic gravel piles, but Silver Creek offers some beautiful flowers for your effort. By following the creek around to the northeast you can avoid much of the loose scree.

Redcloud Peak

14,034

From the Top: The most striking view is the vivid red rock on the summit with the twin towers of Wetterhorn and Uncompahgre in the distance. To the south across the Continental Divide is the prominent Rio Grande Pyramid.

Sunshine Peak

14,001

From the Top: See how many old mining roads you can spot from this summit. Carson, a ghost town, is but five miles southeast, just below the Continental Divide.

The ridge of the Continental Divide provides many good vantage points; this one above Carson looks across the Lake Fork of the Gunnison Valley to Sunshine and Redcloud.

About a mile east of Cinnamon Pass a snow-fringed alpine tarn reflects a white Handies Peak.

American Basin ●

Flowers, flowers, flowers!!! American Basin is renown for its mid-summer beauty. A detour to Sloan Lake is also worth the effort.

Grizzly Gulch ●

A Sawatch-like route of timber, talus, and ptarmigan. Stop to smell the flowers along the way.

Handies Peak

14,048

From the Top: Twenty miles to the south are the Needle Mountains and Grenadier Range. Arrow and Vestal in the Grenadiers are the most spectacular with Pigeon Peak at the west end of the Needles also prominent. Closer is a steep headwall just above Sloan Lake at the south end of American Basin. If you look east between Redcloud and Sunshine, San Luis Peak appears as a bump on the horizon.

The blue-green waters of Sloan Lake tempt the visitor to upper American Basin, west of Handies Peak.

Sneffels Range and San Miguel Mountains

Sneffels Range

One of Colorado's infrequent east-west ranges has but a single fourteener. However, there are many other significant summits including Dallas, Gilpin, Teakettle, Potosi, and Whitehouse, all above 13,000 feet. Dallas and Teakettle are Century summits. Like all the ranges of the greater San Juans, mining was instrumental in creating the roads we use today. Camp Bird, on the way to Yankee Boy Basin, is one of the ten largest mines in the state. It operates even today, if only on an intermittent basis.

The rich volcanic soils coupled with abundant moisture make the flowers of this region legendary. Late July is the flower season and the basins filled with flowers line up in a string of interesting place names. Imogene, Silver, Sidney, Governor, and Yankee Boy Basins beckon your camera and will reward the craftsman with superior results.

A once-stout horse barn along the Bilk Basin access road provides an asymmetric frame for Wilson Peak.

San Miguel Mountains

The San Miguels are both beautiful and dangerous. This volcanic range is characterized by brittle steep rock. When climbing, any rock you grab as a handhold can be yours to own. Having a multi-hundred pound boulder as a keepsake is the last thing you need when moving up a steep rock face. Briskly step out of the way, inasmuch as gravity works very well at these altitudes.

Another aspect of volcanic rock is the color. Unlike the predominant grays of the metamorphic gneiss and schist of the Sawatch, rust red is a common color in the San Miguel Range. This rock is rich in minerals which at the forest level provide an abundant plant population. Grassy alpine meadows are not to be seen, likely due to the continuing flaking off of rock from nearby cliffs. Upper Kilpacker, Navajo and Silver Pick Basins are rock-strewn wastelands.

Summit	Elevation	Rank	Page
Mount Sneffels	14,150	28	101
Wilson Peak	14,017	48	103
Mount Wilson	14,246	16	105
El Diente Peak	14,159	24	105

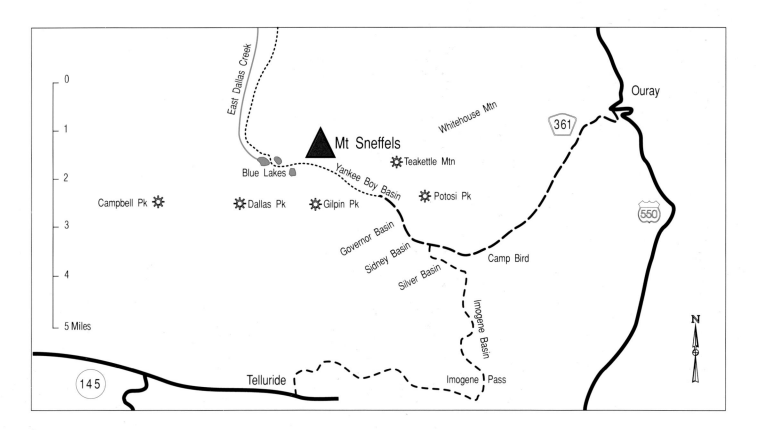

A beaver pond on East Dallas Creek reflects golden aspen and Mount Sneffels.

Yankee Boy Basin ◆

A combination of roads and good trails lead to the base, followed by a steep gravel gully and an even steeper snow gully to the summit.

Blue Lakes ◆

A more scenic, less-traveled approach which circles around the west side with the same final approach as Yankee Boy.

Mount Sneffels

14,150

From the Top: The blue-green waters of the Blue Lakes shimmer 3000 feet below. Up the other side of this compact valley is Dallas Peak, Colorado's hardest Century peak. Twenty miles away is the imposing bulk of Uncompahgre Peak. Notice how Wetterhorn Peak is framed by the larger, slightly more distant Uncompahgre.

The main climbing gulleys of Mount Sneffels are visible from Governor Basin with the Mountain Top Mine in the foreground.

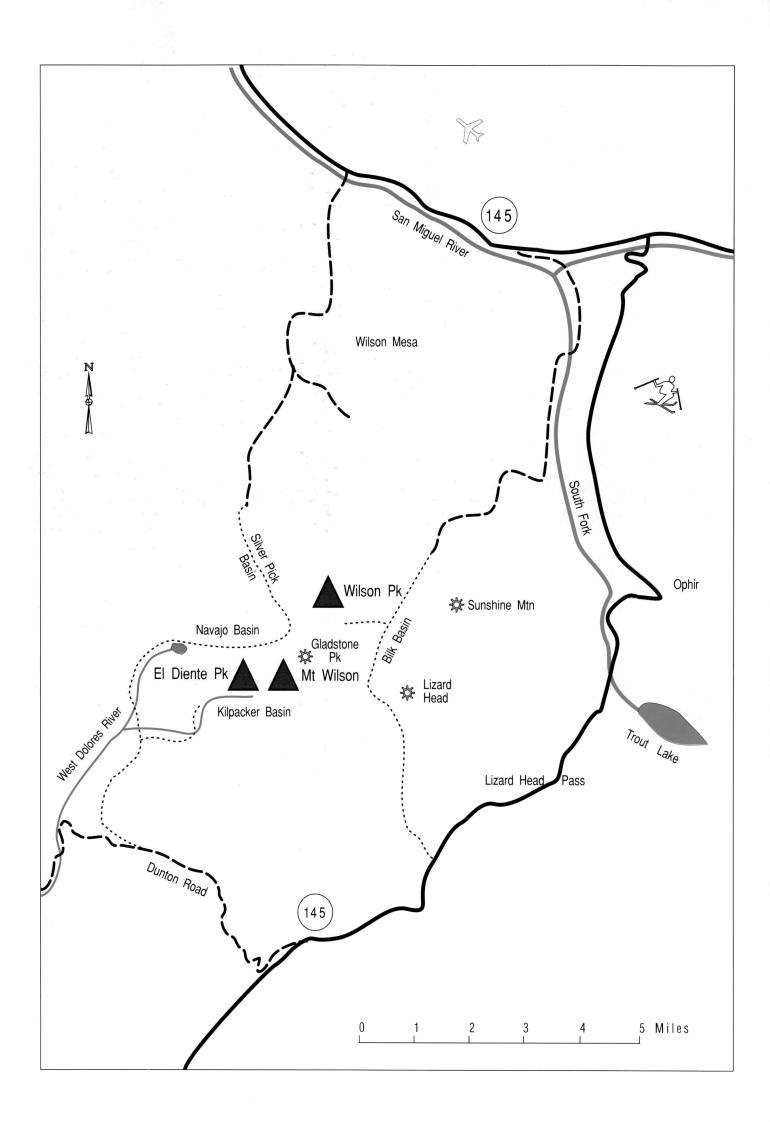

145

San Miguel River

Wilson Mesa

N

Silver Pick Basin

Wilson Pk.

Sunshine Mtn

South Fork

Ophir

Navajo Basin

Gladstone Pk

Bilk Basin

El Diente Pk

Mt Wilson

Lizard Head

West Dolores River

Kilpacker Basin

Trout Lake

Lizard Head Pass

Dunton Road

145

0   1   2   3   4   5   Miles

Wilson Peak is part of a panorama which swings from Navajo Pass around to Gladstone Peak. As seen from the summit of Mount Wilson. Read the Mount Wilson text and see if you can spot the described features.

Silver Pick Basin ◆

Loose talus is the most notable feature of this basin. Expect difficult climbing with some exposure near the summit.

Bilk Basin ◆

A totally different, longer approach which uses the same final route to the summit. Expect many fewer people until the summit ridge.

Wilson Peak

14,017

From the Top: Looking over the south ridge of Wilson Peak are the triple summits of Gladstone, Mount Wilson and El Diente with Navajo Basin below the ridge. Further right is Navajo Pass and Silver Pick Basin. To the north is Wilson Mesa which abruptly drops into the San Miguel River. Across the river are the south slopes of the Sneffels Range with Mount Sneffels further to the right. The twisting slopes of the Telluride Ski Area are visible to the northeast. Ophir Pass can be located by the road which crosses the west face of Lookout Peak. Further right is the volcanic plug of Lizard Head Peak. Between Lizard Head and Wilson Peak is Bilk Basin. See if you can spot the small cabin high in Bilk Basin.

Mount Wilson and El Diente from just below the summit of Wilson Peak. The terrain just below and right of the dog is the difficult portion of the Wilson Peak route.

Navajo Pass ◆◆

The longest, most difficult, and most popular route for Mount Wilson. Its popularity is largely due to the possibility for strong parties to conquer all three summits in one day.

Navajo Lake ◆◆

A rocky wilderness lake is the start for a difficult climb. This side of the San Miguels has abundant flowers in late summer.

Kilpacker Creek ◆

The easiest route for El Diente and Mount Wilson, but making all three in one day is not within reach.

Mount Wilson

14,246

From the Top: Wilson's small steep summit permits bird-like looks all around. The steep permanent snowfield east of the summit is one of the last remaining in Colorado. How long before it disappears and becomes seasonal? The rocky rubble of Kilpacker Basin is to the west, with the connecting ridge to El Diente slightly to the north. Looking north you will see Navajo Pass and Wilson Peak. Further right is Sneffels, just left of Gladstone.

El Diente Peak

14,159

From the Top: Look south to see Dunton Meadows just past the tree-covered ridge. Kilpacker Creek is just below El Diente and flows into the West Dolores River. From left to right Dolores Peak, Lone Cone and Little Cone are visible. The western horizon reveals the blue-gray outline of Utah's La Sal Mountains.

El Diente as seen from high on the west flanks of Mount Wilson's south false summit. The view looks west down Kilpacker Basin and shows most of the traverse route between Mount Wilson and El Diente Peak.

Needle Mountains

In the midst of the most rugged and inaccessible portion of the San Juans are the Needle Mountains. Beyond the attraction of the summits is the high probability of encountering the resident herd of mountain goats.

A herd numbering at a dozen or more occupies the terra above timberline. Their numbers will consist mostly of nannies, kids, and yearlings, possibly a single billy. The Twin Lakes are a favorite haunt at midday. Because they are so curious, an unguarded open tent is just so much shredded nylon as their horns hook on the way out. Perhaps you will be treated, as I was, to a rock dance on the Sidewalk in the Sky. All our fancy hi-tech footwear is humbled by what evolution has provided these animals.

Chicago Basin is the only practical way to climb the three Needle fourteeners. There are numerous ways to get to Chicago Basin, all of which involve considerable hiking. Some add the mystique of a train ride.

Train Routes

The train routes parallel the Animas River. Two possibilities use coal-fired steam locomotives and the third is diesel powered. Reservations are recommended for the busy summer months. The steam trains carry you as a normal passenger and place your packs in a boxcar. Some tickets are interchangeable—inquire. All trains drop passengers at Needleton, 8135 feet. Lest you think that Needleton is a train station, picture a rail siding instead . . . no creature comforts here.

Hiking Access

Needleton to Chicago Basin

The most popular route starts at the Needleton train siding and follows the old wagon road along Needle Creek to Chicago Basin. It's about six miles and a 3000 foot elevation gain to lower Chicago Basin, at 11,000 feet. Numerous campsites exist in the timber on either side of the creek. No camp fires are permitted in the Needle Creek drainage, just stoves. Strong parties may wish to camp at the twin lakes, 12,500 feet. The last 500 feet to the lakes is very steep.

Columbine Pass

A multi-day backpack which covers sixteen miles one-way and crosses 12,800 foot Columbine Pass. Excellent trails in Colorado's largest wilderness area ease your journey.

Purgatory

You start at Purgatory Ski Area and backpack 10 miles along the Animas River to Needle Creek. From there the route is the same as Needleton to Chicago Basin.

Summit	Elevation	Rank	Page
Mount Eolus	14,083	33	109
Sunlight Peak	14,059	39	109
Windom Peak	14,082	34	109

Sunlight and Windom as seen from west of the Twin Lakes.

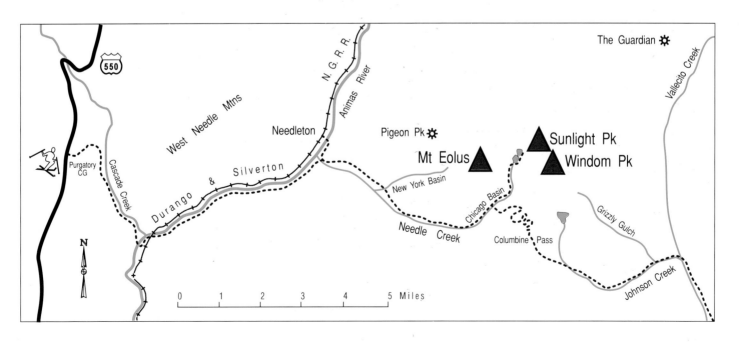

Sunlight from Windom with the dark forms of Arrow and Vestal in the nearby Grenadiers.

Eolus ◆

The Sidewalk in the Sky is the highlight of this summit. Great rock, and top-of-the-world views. If the goats are on the sidewalk, go slow so as not to scare them away.

Sunlight ◆

The lower part is steep, loose scree followed by narrow catwalk shelves. Near the summit a short steep pitch puts you into position for a belly-crawl under a rock plate. Great fun!

Windom ◆

A ridge of large solid boulders with minor exposure leads to the crest. A short scamper to the south places you on the small flat summit with great views.

The summit of Sunlight consists of a large stone block and a smaller leaning plate. These two objects create the frame for this photo of Eolus and North Eolus.

Mount Eolus

14,083

From the Top: Look west for the best views. Much of the Animas River can be seen as a silver thread beneath great canyon walls. Purgatory Ski Area can be seen as a series of light green grassy slopes contrasting with the dark green forest. Nearby Pigeon Peak is the most prominent of the Needle Mountains and the fourth highest.

Sunlight Peak

14,059

From the Top: Sunlight has two tops, the highest point which is a large plate leaning against a rounded boulder; and the more ordinary rock summit 50 feet south which has the USGS benchmark. To the north are the twin summits of Arrow and Vestal, the monarchs of the Grenadiers. Far to the east is the lonesome Rio Grande Pyramid. Below are glacier-carved lakes in the high-alpine Sunlight Basin.

Windom Peak

14,082

From the Top: Southeast of the summit are several blue-green lakes in upper Grizzly Gulch. The near vertical east side of Windom induces some involuntary knee quiver. To the southwest the Chicago Basin is exposed with its trail system and infrequent mines.

Fourteeners by Difficulty

Very Difficult ◆◆

Mount Wilson	14,246	Capitol Peak	14,130	North Maroon Peak	14,014
Crestone Needle	14,197	Little Bear Peak	14,037		

Difficult ◆

Crestone Peak	14,294	Mount Sneffels	14,150	Pyramid Peak	14,018
Longs Peak	14,255	Snowmass Mountain	14,092	Wilson Peak	14,017
Kit Carson Mountain	14,165	Mount Eolus	14,083	Wetterhorn Peak	14,015
El Diente Peak	14,159	Windom Peak	14,082		
Maroon Peak	14,156	Sunlight Peak	14,059		

Moderate ■

Mount Harvard	14,420	Mount Belford	14,197	Ellingwood Point	14,042
Blanca Peak	14,345	Mount Yale	14,196	Mount Lindsey	14,042
La Plata Peak	14,336	Mount Tabeguache	14,155	Redcloud Peak	14,034
Uncompahgre Peak	14,309	Mount Oxford	14,153	Mount of the Holy Cross	14,005
Castle Peak	14,265	Missouri Mountain	14,067	Sunshine Peak	14,001
Mount Shavano	14,229	Humboldt Peak	14,064		

Easy ●

Mount Elbert	14,433	Mount Evans	14,264	Handies Peak	14,048
Mount Massive	14,421	Mount Princeton	14,197	Culebra Peak	14,047
Mount Lincoln	14,286	Mount Bross	14,172	Mount Sherman	14,036
Grays Peak	14,270	Mount Democrat	14,148	San Luis Peak	14,014
Mount Antero	14,269	Pikes Peak	14,110	Huron Peak	14,005
Torreys Peak	14,267	Mount Columbia	14,073		
Quandary Peak	14,265	Mount Bierstadt	14,060		

Fourteeners by Elevation

1	Mount Elbert	14,433	18	Mount Belford	14,197	37	Humboldt Peak	14,064
2	Mount Massive	14,421	18	Mount Princeton	14,197	38	Mount Bierstadt	14,060
3	Mount Harvard	14,420	21	Mount Yale	14,196	39	Sunlight Peak	14,059
4	Blanca Peak	14,345	22	Mount Bross	14,172	40	Handies Peak	14,048
5	La Plata Peak	14,336	23	Kit Carson Mountain	14,165	41	Culebra Peak	14,047
6	Uncompahgre Peak	14,309	24	El Diente Peak	14,159	42	Ellingwood Point	14,042
7	Crestone Peak	14,294	25	Maroon Peak	14,156	42	Mount Lindsey	14,042
8	Mount Lincoln	14,286	26	Mount Tabeguache	14,155	44	Little Bear Peak	14,037
9	Grays Peak	14,270	27	Mount Oxford	14,153	45	Mount Sherman	14,036
10	Mount Antero	14,269	28	Mount Sneffels	14,150	46	Redcloud Peak	14,034
11	Torreys Peak	14,267	29	Mount Democrat	14,148	47	Pyramid Peak	14,018
12	Castle Peak	14,265	30	Capitol Peak	14,130	48	Wilson Peak	14,017
12	Quandary Peak	14,265	31	Pikes Peak	14,110	49	Wetterhorn Peak	14,015
14	Mount Evans	14,264	32	Snowmass Mountain	14,092	50	North Maroon Peak	14,014
15	Longs Peak	14,255	33	Mount Eolus	14,083	50	San Luis Peak	14,014
16	Mount Wilson	14,246	34	Windom Peak	14,082	52	Huron Peak	14,005
17	Mount Shavano	14,229	35	Mount Columbia	14,073	52	Mount of the Holy Cross	14,005
18	Crestone Needle	14,197	36	Missouri Mountain	14,067	54	Sunshine Peak	14,001

A ragtag army of shedding goats around the Twin Lakes with Sunlight Peak looming above.

Top: Morning clouds give way to blue skies on the Sidewalk in the Sky as a climber approaches Mount Eolus.

Above: Mid-day clouds float between Kit Carson Mountain and its many high summits, as seen from the summit of Crestone Needle.

Right: Lingering morning fog surrounds the summit of Mount Wilson as seen from its south false summit.